Holidays Around the World

Celebrate
Independence
Day

Deborah Heiligman
Consultant, Dr. Matthew Dennis

NATIONAL GEOGRAPHIC
WASHINGTON, D.C.

Carla Villareal celebrates at the Fourth of July parade in Seguin, Texas.

parades

Every July 4th people all over the United States celebrate Independence Day. We celebrate with parades, picnics, and fireworks.

We celebrate the birth of our country, the United States of America.

< Corn on the cob

picnics

< American flag

fireworks

We remember how

∧ *Two boys dress up as American colonists in a special Independence Day event at the American Museum in Bath, England.*

On Independence Day, we remember how our country was born. A long time ago, the land we live in was not called the United States. It was not one country. Native Americans lived here, and each tribe had its own nation and government. Then people from European countries came and settled here. They fought the Indians and pushed many of them West.

By the 1700s, most of the eastern part of this land was ruled by Great Britain. There were 13 British colonies. Many colonists came to feel that Great Britain was not ruling them fairly. They decided to break away. Fighting began in 1775, with General George Washington leading the army.

∨ *In Mendham, New Jersey, men dressed as Revolutionary War soldiers fire muskets during a Fourth of July parade.*

our country was born.

The Second Continental Congress met in Philadelphia, Pennsylvania, in the summer of 1776. The Congress represented the 13 colonies. They decided there should be a document that declared why they wanted to be independent. So Thomas Jefferson wrote the Declaration of Independence. It was adopted on July 4, 1776. That week the declaration was read aloud—to cheers and celebration.

July 4th is our country's birthday.

Although it took five years to win the War for Independence (which is also called the Revolutionary War), July 4th is the day we became a country. That's why we celebrate our country's birthday on the Fourth of July.

< *Children look at an original copy of the Declaration of Independence on display at the National Constitution Center in Philadelphia, Pennsylvania.*

And do we celebrate! All over the country Americans celebrate in big ways and small ways. People whose families have been here for 300 years or more celebrate. People who just moved here from other countries celebrate.

We dress in red,

white, and blue.

∧ *Emma DeVries, her dad, and a friend decorate Emma's home in Lincoln, Nebraska, with red, white, and blue banners.*

< *Native Americans enjoy July 4th in Anchorage, Alaska. Not all American Indians celebrate this holiday. For some of us it is a day to protest the loss of our native lands.*

We celebrate what our country stands for: liberty, equality, justice, and freedom for all. We fly flags. We dress in red, white, and blue, the colors of our flag.

> Boy scouts in Edmond, Oklahoma, carry a giant U.S. flag in a parade.

We have parades.

< Kandi the dachshund shows her Independence Day patriotism in Springfield, Missouri.

In many towns and cities

the day starts off with a parade.
We have little parades; we have big
parades. Soldiers who fought for our
country march. Children march.
Bands play patriotic songs. We wave
our flags, we cheer, we sing along.

> Caleb Brening (left) and Trace Bowen
ride unicycles in the Patriots Parade
in Hutchinson, Kansas.

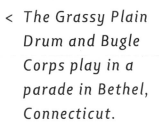

< The Grassy Plain
Drum and Bugle
Corps play in a
parade in Bethel,
Connecticut.

< American soldiers in Baghdad, Iraq, celebrate the Fourth of July with a cookout.

V Friends Carolyn Stark and Matthew Palacio enjoy red, white, and blue ice pops at a backyard cookout in Katonah, New York.

Picnics!

∧ Mary Frampton, wearing a Statue of Liberty hat, laughs with her friends at an Independence Day picnic in McClellanville, South Carolina.

∧ An all-American hot dog

Since the Fourth of July is in the summertime, we spend the day outside. We go to the beach or the lake or pool.

We have picnics and cookouts. We eat hot dogs, hamburgers, pickles, and chips. We eat deviled eggs and corn on the cob. We eat watermelon and ice cream and strawberry shortcake. People from different countries add foods from their homelands, too. We are free to eat whatever we want!

We have fun traditions.

> *Kids compete in a watermelon-eating contest in Long Beach, California.*

We have many Independence

Day traditions. Some of them are silly, like food-eating contests. On Coney Island in New York, there has been a hot dog eating contest on the Fourth of July almost every year since 1916!

We have musical traditions. We go to concerts. We listen to big orchestras play patriotic songs. We sing our national anthem.

< The Lemhi County Fair in Idaho is a great place to celebrate Independence Day.

We also have sports

traditions. We run races. We play games. And the Fourth of July is a perfect day to go to a baseball game, a great American tradition!

We play.

∧ *Councilman Duane Pomeroy tries to catch a water balloon at an Independence Day celebration in Topeka, Kansas.*

> *Kids play tug-of-war at the Jamaican Association Fourth of July picnic in San Francisco, California.*

< Tyler Stevens and his dad cool off with friends on Independence Day in Griswold, Connecticut.

> Little League baseball players in Bend, Oregon, react to an umpire's call during an all-star game held Fourth of July weekend.

People make speeches.

∧ *At Monticello, the historic home of Thomas Jefferson in Charlottesville, Virginia, Judge James H. Michael, Jr., swears in 77 people as United States citizens on July 4, 2003.*

We hear speeches on Independence Day, too. This is a tradition that goes back to the American Revolution. Back then people made speeches against Great Britain and for independence. Today, politicians make speeches and meet voters.

> *Many people take the oath of citizenship on Independence Day, such as this woman in Seattle, Washington.*

v *In New York City, Julian Davis reads part of the Declaration of Independence at a ceremony to honor victims of the terrorist attacks of September 11, 2001.*

People fighting for rights also make speeches, often about freedom and equality. This also goes back to the time of the American Revolution, when some people began to argue that slaves should be freed.

We think about what our country stands for. We think about how we can make our country better.

We watch fireworks!

When night falls we have the grandest tradition of all: We watch fireworks! All over the country the night sky lights up with brilliant colors and fantastic displays—birthday candles exploding in the sky! The sounds of the fireworks remind us of the war long ago in which we fought for independence. The beauty reminds us of the ideals of the United States of America.

< *Fourth of July fireworks light up the sky over the Philadelphia Museum of Art in Philadelphia, Pennsylvania.*

< *Collin Erickson salutes at a parade in Clatskanie, Oregon.*

We remember.

∧ At a park in New York City, people look at a large American flag made up of individual quilt panels honoring those who died in the attacks of September 11, 2001.

< War veterans march in an Independence Day parade held in Brandon, Vermont.

As we celebrate with our family

and friends, we think about the Declaration of Independence. We remember the words that we keep trying to make true:

"We hold these Truths to be self-evident, that all Men are created equal, that they are endowed by their Creator with certain unalienable Rights, that among these are Life, Liberty and the Pursuit of Happiness."

On the Fourth of July we celebrate our country. We celebrate the people who make up our country. We celebrate equality. We celebrate opportunity. We celebrate freedom. Hooray for freedom!

Hooray for freedom!

At Gasworks Park in Seattle, Washington, families fly kites together near an inflated Statue of Liberty on the Fourth of July.

MORE ABOUT INDEPENDENCE DAY

Contents

∧ *A three-legged race in Florida*

Just the Facts

WHO CELEBRATES IT: Americans celebrate U.S. Independence Day. People around the world celebrate their own independence days.

WHAT: A cheerful holiday that emphasizes freedom, equality, patriotism, and togetherness.

WHEN: July 4.

HOW LONG: One day, although if the Fourth falls on or near a weekend, people often make a longer holiday out of it.

RITUALS: Parades; patriotic speeches; picnics; decorating with flags and banners; fireworks.

FOOD: Picnic foods, including corn on the cob, deviled eggs, hot dogs, and hamburgers. Also cakes with red, white, and blue icing.

A Three-Legged Race

Three-legged races are a July 4th picnic tradition. Why? Because they're fun! But also because a three-legged race requires cooperation, teamwork, and perseverance—just like the founding of our country did.

1. Mark a start line and a finish line.

2. Divide everyone into pairs.

3. Tie the two inside ankles together with a scarf or a rope—not too tight! Don't leave strings hanging down. Or you can put both legs into a pillow case or burlap sack.

4. On your mark, get set, go! The first pair to get to the finish line—with three legs—wins!

Independence Days Around the World

Just as the American colonies gained independence from Great Britain and became the United States of America, over the years colonies and territories throughout the world have gained independence and become countries. People in those nations celebrate their independence days much like we celebrate ours. And people from those countries who live in the United States often celebrate two independence days—the U.S. Fourth of July and the one from their land of origin. Here are a few examples:

In **Mexico,** independence from Spain is celebrated on September 16 with a big fiesta! People buy flags, balloons, sombreros, and banners in green, white, and red, the national colors. Many people wear traditional dress, and mariachi bands play traditional Mexican music. Children break piñatas and eat candy. Many people in the United States celebrate Mexican Independence Day, and some also celebrate Cinco de Mayo (Fifth of May). That date commemorates a victory of the Mexican army against the French and Austrians.

In **Iceland,** independence from Denmark is celebrated on June 17 with parades, music, dancing, and lots of candy for kids! On September 30, people in the African nation of **Botswana** celebrate their nation's independence from British rule with music, speeches, fireworks, and parties. In **Cambodia,** people celebrate freedom from France on November 9. Soldiers march, politicians and the King make speeches, and children wave flags. Some independence days are somber, or serious, as people think of those who died fighting for freedom. Some are cheerful. But all celebrate the same thing: the right to be free.

∨ *Children wave Cambodian flags in Phnom Penh on Cambodian Independence Day, which is celebrated on November 9.*

Kay's Deviled Eggs

This recipe is from my friend Kay Winters. (Be sure to have an adult help you at the stove.)

INGREDIENTS:
8 eggs
4 tablespoons mayonnaise
2 teaspoons dried mustard
1 tablespoon horseradish, or to taste.
Dill for sprinkling

1. Put eggs in saucepan. Cover with cold water.

2. Bring to a boil, with the pot uncovered.

3. Turn off heat, cover pot, and let sit for 30 minutes.

4. Run cold water over eggs to cool.

5. Gently crack the shells, then peel eggs.

6. Slice eggs in half and remove yolks to bowl.

7. Mash yolks, then add mayonnaise, mustard, and horseradish. Mix well.

8. Spoon yolk mixture into egg whites. Sprinkle with dill. Refrigerate the deviled eggs until time to serve.

Myths and Facts

MYTH: We celebrate Independence Day on July 4, because that's when Congress declared independence.

FACT: Congress declared independence on July 2. The Declaration of Independence was adopted (after lots of editing by Congress members) on July 4. Copies were printed that day.

MYTH: The Declaration of Independence was signed by all the delegates on July 4, 1776.

FACT: The delegates began to sign the Declaration of Independence on August 2, 1776.

MYTH: The Liberty Bell in Philadelphia's Independence Hall was rung at the first public reading of the Declaration of Independence on July 4, 1776.

FACT: The first public reading of the Declaration of Independence was on July 8, 1776. (It had to be printed first.) When people heard the declaration, they accepted it, and proclaimed it throughout the land. Bells were rung on July 8, but historians now doubt that the Liberty Bell was one of them. The steeple of the State House it was in was in bad condition then. By the way, the Liberty Bell was not called the Liberty Bell until 1839.

MYTH: Both Thomas Jefferson and John Adams died on July 4.

FACT: It's true! Both men—signers of the Declaration of Independence and Presidents of the United States—died on July 4, 1826, exactly 50 years after the adoption of the Declaration.

Find Out More

BOOKS

Those with a star (*) are especially good for children.

Dennis, Matthew. *Red, White, and Blue Letter Days: An American Calendar.* Cornell University Press, 2002. A wonderful book that examines the history of our American holidays and how we shaped them. Chapter one is "Political Fireworks: American Independence Day, 1776-2000."

*Giblin, James Cross. *Fireworks, Picnics, and Flags: The Story of the Fourth of July Symbols.* Clarion Books, 1983. Although this book is old, it is filled with interesting historical information and is very well-written. It Is good for older children (9-12).

*Hess, Debra. *The Fourth of July.* Benchmark Books, Marshall Cavendish, 2004. An excellent book about the history, symbols, and celebrations of the Fourth of July.

*Hoig, Stan. *It's the Fourth of July!* Cobble Hill Books, Dutton, 1995. A very good and thoughtful book about the history of Independence Day. It includes the Declaration of Independence. This is good for older children (9-12).

WEB SITES

There are many sites about Independence Day. Here are some of my favorites.

http://www.american.edu/heintze/fourth.htm
This is a huge site called the Fourth of July Celebrations Database. It has, among other things, links to celebrations all over the country.

http://www.archives.gov/national-archives-experience/charters/declaration.html
This site, about the Declaration of Independence, is put out by the government. The National Archives site is great for researching a topic in American history.

http://www.loc.gov/exhibits/declara/declara1.html
Another really good government site (the Library of Congress) about the declaration.

http://usinfo.state.gov/scv/life_and_culture/holidays/july_4.html
One more government site about the Fourth of July.

http://www.duke.edu/eng169s2/group1/lex3/firstpge.htm
The Declaration of Independence Home Page.

∧ *A rough draft of Thomas Jefferson's Declaration of Independence*

http://en.wikipedia.org/wiki/Independence_days
This site has a list of most of the Independence Days celebrated around the world.

MOVIE

1776. This is a fun movie about the drafting of the Declaration of Independence. It is not completely accurate, but it will give you a good idea of what happened. The last scene, where they all sign the declaration right then—not true. But it is moving!

Glossary

Colonies: More than one colony. A colony is a group of people who leave their country to settle in a new place. It is also the place where those people have settled. The people who are settled there are called colonists.

Congress: A group of leaders elected to represent the people and make laws.

Declaration: The act of announcing something, or the announcement itself.

Document: A piece of paper that contains important information.

Independence: The state of being free from the control of other people or things.

Patriotic: Showing love for your country.

Revolution: A complete change. A revolution is also a war or movement that ends one government or kind of rule and creates a new and different sort of government.

Unalienable (also inalienable): Not able to be taken away.

Where This Book's Photos Were Taken

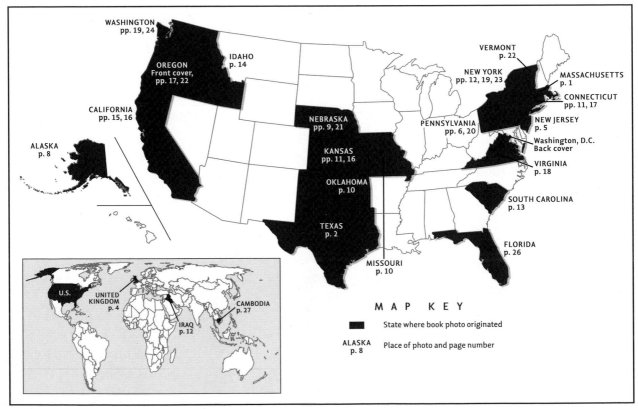

WASHINGTON pp. 19, 24

IDAHO p. 14

OREGON Front cover, pp. 17, 22

CALIFORNIA pp. 15, 16

ALASKA p. 8

NEBRASKA pp. 9, 21

KANSAS pp. 11, 16

OKLAHOMA p. 10

TEXAS p. 2

MISSOURI p. 10

VERMONT p. 22

NEW YORK pp. 12, 19, 23

MASSACHUSETTS p. 1

CONNECTICUT pp. 11, 17

PENNSYLVANIA pp. 6, 20

NEW JERSEY p. 5

Washington, D.C. Back cover

VIRGINIA p. 18

SOUTH CAROLINA p. 13

FLORIDA p. 26

U.S.

UNITED KINGDOM p. 4

CAMBODIA p. 27

IRAQ p. 12

MAP KEY

■ State where book photo originated

ALASKA p. 8 Place of photo and page number

The United States: Born and Reborn on the Fourth of July

by Dr. Matthew Dennis

On the Fourth of July, Americans enthusiastically celebrate their nation's birth. The day's signal event—fireworks exploding in the heavens—suggests both the war that won American independence and the joyful abandon that traditionally marks the holiday. In 1776, with Congressional adoption and then boisterous public acclamation of the Declaration of Independence, Americans literally celebrated themselves into existence as a new nation. And they have been doing so ever since.

Declaring independence was a revolutionary act. And a "decent respect to the opinions of mankind" demanded an explanation. The Declaration of Independence thus clarified for Americans and the world, "We hold these truths to be self-evident, that all men are created equal, that they are endowed by their Creator with certain unalienable Rights, that among these are Life, Liberty and the pursuit of Happiness." Thomas Jefferson's text would go on to assert the rights of self-government and revolution, indict King George III, and formally decree independence. But those words proclaiming human equality blasted off the page like a firecracker and remained conspicuous and percussive throughout American history.

Independence Day is always festive, and in the best of times it is easy and fitting to lose ourselves in the joys of food, fun, and fanfare. Parades, picnics, and pyrotechnics are appropriate for the country's birthday. Yet, amid these pleasures, the holiday has always been political, even revolutionary, as diverse Americans define themselves and lay claim to the promise of equality on the Fourth of July.

The American Revolution failed to abolish slavery in the United States, but immediately African Americans and anti-slavery advocates argued for freedom and protested slavery in terms supplied by the declaration. In an 1852 holiday oration, the great abolitionist Frederick Douglass continued to press the embarrassing question, "What to the Slave is the Fourth of July?" Women too demanded equal rights in language inspired by the Declaration, arguing at Seneca Falls in 1848 that "all men and women are created equal." Until late in the 19th century, Independence Day served as the country's Labor Day, a suitable moment to promote economic as well as political democracy. For working people, the Fourth became a different sort of Independence Day, a time to take a holiday, without their employers' permission, and to "strike" out in protests, walking out of workplaces and marching in their own parades. Simply indulging in recreation and leisure on the Fourth of July, in an era of relentless toil in factories or farms, could be an important political act. Our own Independence Day festivity today, though oblivious to this history, is nonetheless an apt tribute to the struggles for freedom, opportunity, and prosperity achieved at so great a cost. Acknowledging that travail can make our celebrations sweeter.

Mostly, the Fourth of July serves a unifying purpose, bringing Americans together as they embrace the country's common ideals and claim a legitimate place on the parade route. It is a time when diverse Americans can celebrate themselves into first-class citizenship, joining the national potluck and enhancing it with their own, unique contributions. On no other day do so many new citizens take their oaths of allegiance. No holiday is more important in symbolizing why the country is worthy of such allegiance.

Matthew Dennis is Professor of History at the University of Oregon in Eugene. He is the author of Red, White, and Blue Letter Days: An American Calendar.

For Talia Weiner, a real firecracker, born on the Fourth of July!

PICTURE CREDITS

1: ©Jonathan Sachs/ipnstock.com; 2-3: ©Bob Owen/San Antonio Express/ZUMA Press; 3 up: khwi/Shutterstock; 3 lo: Faithworks Communications House/ Shutterstock; 4: ©Aaron Schuman; 5: ©Mike Yamashita/ Woodfin Camp/ipnstock.com; 6: ©Tim Shaffer/Reuters; 8: ©Paul Souders/ipnstock.com; 9: ©Joel Sartore; 10 up: ©Brian Terry/ The Oklahoman/ Associated Press; 10 lo: ©Dean Curtis/The News Leader/ Associated Press; 11 up: ©Travis Morisse/ The Hutchinson News/ Associated Press; 11 lo: ©Gabe Palmer/Alamy Ltd; 12 up: ©Wally Santana/ Associated Press; 12 lo: ©Gabe Palacio/ipnstock.com; 13 up: ©Alan Hawes/ the Post and Courier/ Associated Press; 13 lo: Dawid Konopka/Shutterstock; 14: ©Joel Sartore; 15: ©Kayte Deioma\PhotoEdit, Inc.; 16 up: ©Chris Landsberger/Topeka Capital Journal/Associated Press; 16 lo: ©Rachel Epstein/PhotoEdit, Inc; 17 up: ©Khoi Ton/ The Norwich Bulletin/ Associated Press; 17 lo: ©Diane Kulpinski;18: ©Andrew Shurtleff/ The Daily Progress/Associated Press; 19 up: ©Paul Souders/ipnstock.com; 19 lo; ©Michael J. Doolittle/The Image Works; 20: ©Bob Krist; 21: ©Joel Sartore; 22 up: ©Roger Werth/ The Daily News/Associated Press; 22 lo: ©Caleb Kenna/ipnstock.com; 23: ©Peter Morgan/Reuters; 24-25: ©Paul Souders/ipnstock.com; 26: ©Paul Barton/Corbis; 27: ©Andy Eames/Associated Press; 28: ©Marfé Ferguson Delano; 29: Library of Congress.

Text copyright © 2007 Deborah Heiligman

Published by the National Geographic Society.
All rights reserved. Reproduction of the whole or any part of the contents without written permission from the National Geographic Society is strictly prohibited. For information about special discounts for bulk purchases, contact National Geographic Special Sales: ngspecsales@ngs.org.

Library of Congress Cataloging-in-Publication Data

Heiligman, Deborah.
  Celebrate Independence Day / Deborah Heiligman ; consultant, Matthew Dennis.
    p. cm. -- (Holidays around the world)
  Includes bibliographical references and index.
  ISBN 978-1-4263-0074-5 (trade : alk. paper) -- ISBN 978-1-4263-0075-2 (library : alk. paper)
  1. Fourth of July celebrations--Juvenile literature. 2. Fourth of July--Juvenile literature. I. Dennis, Matthew, 1955- II. Title.
E286.A12835 2007
394.2634--dc22
                    2006100316

Front cover: Decked out in red, white, and blue, people line the street for the Independence Day parade in Independence, Oregon. *Back cover:* Spectators watch fireworks from the grounds of the Washington Monument in Washington, D.C., on the Fourth of July. *Title page:* A boy in Boston celebrates the Fourth of July with a patriotic cap.

One of the world's largest nonprofit scientific and educational organizations, the National Geographic Society was founded in 1888 "for the increase and diffusion of geographic knowledge." Fulfilling this mission, the Society educates and inspires millions every day through its magazines, books, television programs, videos, maps and atlases, research grants, the National Geographic Bee, teacher workshops, and innovative classroom materials. The Society is supported through membership dues, charitable gifts, and income from the sale of its educational products. This support is vital to National Geographic's mission to increase global understanding and promote conservation of our planet through exploration, research, and education. For more information, please call 1-800-NGS-LINE (647-5463) or write to the following address:

NATIONAL GEOGRAPHIC SOCIETY
1145 17th Street N.W., Washington, D.C. 20036-4688 U.S.A.

Visit the Society's Web site at www.nationalgeographic.com.

John M. Fahey, Jr., *President and Chief Executive Officer*
Gilbert M. Grosvenor, *Chairman of the Board*
Nina D. Hoffman, *Executive Vice President; President, Book Publishing Group*

STAFF FOR THIS BOOK

Nancy Laties Feresten, *Vice President, Editor-in-Chief of Children's Books*
Bea Jackson, *Design and Illustrations Director, Children's Books*
Amy Shields, *Executive Editor, Children's Books*
Marfé Ferguson Delano, *Project Editor*
Lori Epstein, *Illustrations Editor*
Melissa Brown, *Project Designer*
Carl Mehler, *Director of Maps*
Priyanka Lamichhane, *Assistant Editor*
Rebecca Baines, *Editorial Assistant*
Jennifer Thornton, *Managing Editor*
R. Gary Colbert, *Production Director*
Lewis R. Bassford, *Production Manager*
Vincent P. Ryan, Maryclare Tracy, Nicole Elliott, *Manufacturing Managers*

Series design by 3+Co. and Jim Hiscott.
The body text in the book is set in Mrs. Eaves.
The display text is Lisboa.

ACKNOWLEDGMENTS

Thanks to Matthew Dennis for his insight, help, and good cheer, and to the wonderful editorial help from Marfé Ferguson Delano and Lori Epstein. Thanks to Kay Winters for sharing the recipe for her delicious deviled eggs. And to Laurie Halse Anderson for another good talk.